T & J HARRISC
Ships of Many Tra(

CW00546654

Published by Mainline & Maritime Ltd,
3 Broadleaze, Upper Seagry, near Chippenham, Wiltshire. SN15 5EY
www.mainlineandmaritime.co.uk
orders@mainlineandmaritime.co.uk - 01275 845012

ISBN: 978-1-900340-38-0

Maritime Memories No. 2

A BRIEF HISTORY

T&J Harrison Ltd was established as a firm of Liverpool shipbrokers in 1853, although the brothers Thomas and James Harrison had an active involvement in the Liverpool shipping scene prior to this date.

Despite its founders' background in the operation of sailing ships, the company was soon operating steamships, its first two such vessels being the GLADIATOR and COGNAC, built in 1860 for the French brandy trade. The company disposed of its final sailing ship in 1889.

In the years prior to World War 1, the company adopted an expansionist philosophy, with trade to the Empire a cornerstone of activity through membership of trade partnerships such as the Calcutta conference and the South Africa conference.

At the outbreak of World War 1, the company owned 56 ships, its peak size when measured by number of vessels, totalling almost 300,000 gross tons. However, the changing nature of merchant shipping meant that this tonnage figure was to be equalled several times in subsequent decades.

The interwar years were ones of rebuilding, replacing the 27 ships lost during WW1, and rebuilding the trade lost during the economic nightmare of the 1930s. By the start of World War 2, 45 ships were in the fleet, but the total tonnage was less than 5% lower than it had been in 1914.

The first Harrison ship lost during World War 2 achieved notoriety by means of the movie screens. The HUNTSMAN was one of the victims of the German pocket battleship ADMIRAL GRAF SPEE, whose exploits and demise were portrayed in the film *Battle of the River Plate*.

In 1945, the company was once again faced with a fleet reduced by the ravages of war, and a changed economic situation. The latter was exacerbated by the trend of newly independent colonies to form their own national shipping lines, in many cases being helped to do so by aid packages from generous "first world" countries and organisations.

To meet these new challenges required innovation on a grand scale. At a technical level, the steamship was phased out, the final ones built for Harrison being the CROFTER and FORESTER of 1951/52, and the motor vessel became the dominant form of propulsion.

New trade patterns were also to be met. The company invested heavily in "heavy lift" vessels and the trade in shipment of bulk products rather than the traditional "genera cargo" routes. The organisational structure behind the shipping industry also had to change, with the old conferences becoming obsolete, and container trades being dominated by consortia of shipping companies such as ACT (of which Harrison was a part) and OCL, which could afford the huge infrastructure costs associated with containerisation.

One particularly notable event in the later history of T&J Harrison concerned their first generation container ship ASTRONOMER. In 1982, this vessel was requisitioned into the South Atlantic Task Force following the sinking of the ATLANTIC CONVEYOR. She never returned to Harrison, being converted into the Royal Fleet Auxiliary ship RELIANT in 1983.

The decline continued however, and in 2000, the company sold its last shipping interest, its share in the NCS consortium, to P&O Nedlloyd. What remained was a logistics company, Harrison Logistics, which itself folded in 2002.

ADMINISTRATOR (8714/58) is pictured at Avonmouth on 3rd August 1969, a little over halfway through her career with Harrison, being sold out of the fleet in 1978 and scrapped later the same year.

the late John Wiltshire

ADVENTURER (8791/60) receives assistance from the local tug fleet of Alexandra Towing as she enters the lock at Swansea in the evening light of 6th October 1969.

the late John Wiltshire

ADVENTURER (8791/60) passes Battery Point, Portishead, outward bound from Avonmouth on 1st May 1971. She was the first Harrison ship to be designed with a heavy lift facility, hence the Stülcken derrick amidships.

Derek Chaplin, Andrew Wiltshire Collection

Our final view of the ADVENTURER (8791/60) shows her in Middlesbrough Dock, with the iconic transporter bridge prominent in the background on 24th May 1976.

Michael Greer

ADVOCATE (8380/71) is reflected in the waters of Royal Edward Dock, Avonmouth, on 14th April 1972. She was in the middle of a two year charter to Harrison, from Hain-Nourse Ltd.

the late John Wiltshire

ASTRONOMER (8150/51) works cargo at R Shed, Durban, in 1969. She had less than a year to go in Harrison's service, being sold to Cypriot owners in 1970.

Trevor Jones, Malcolm Cranfield Collection

Same vessel, same year, but it was a somewhat colder early spring day when ASTRONOMER (8150/51) was photographed at Swansea on 14th March 1969. The name was re-used on a new vessel in 1977.

the late John Wiltshire

AUTHOR (8715/58) at Avonmouth in February 1971. The trans-shipment of cargo to barges tied alongside for onward shipment up the River Severn is another sight lost to containerisation.

Bernard McCall Collection

AUTHOR (8715/58) arrives at the entrance to the Manchester Ship Canal at Eastham on 10th May 1978. Note the containers being carried as deck cargo - a far cry from the containerships of today!

Laurie Schofield

BARRISTER (8366/54) at Avonmouth on 28th December 1968. Like many of her fleetmates, she was built at the Sunderland shipyard of William Doxford and Sons.

Laurie Schofield

BARRISTER (8366/54) sailing from Duncan Dock, Cape Town, in June 1974. Within months she had been sold out of the fleet, to owners registered in Liberia. She survived for a further decade, being scrapped in Spain in 1984.

Trevor Jones, Malcolm Cranfield Collection

BENEFACTOR (11299/71) on the Thames in October 1978. She was purchased by Harrison during construction at Sunderland, having been ordered by a Greek company.

Roy Cressey Collection

BENEFACTOR (11299/71) at Avonmouth. Despite her outdated 'tween deck design, she was not scrapped until 1998, sixteen years after leaving Harrison's service.

the late Richard Parsons, courtesy of John D Hill, Malcolm Cranfield Collection

CRAFTSMAN (6726/47) at Liverpool. She was nearing the end of her 20 year career with Harrison, being scrapped in Taiwan in 1967.

Reg Wilson Collection courtesy of Russell Priest, Malcolm Cranfield Collection

CRAFTSMAN (10219/72) passing Greenock on 24th September 1972. She was almost new at the time of the photograph, having been delivered by Doxford & Son earlier in the year.

Bernard McCall Collection

CRAFTSMAN (10219/72) in Avonmouth. Despite her usefulness as a heavy lift ship, she lasted less than a decade in Harrison service, being sold to Greek owners and renamed FORUM CRAFTSMAN in 1981.

the late Richard Parsons courtesy of John D Hill, Malcolm Cranfield Collection

CROFTER (8377/51) at Avonmouth on 19th February 1971. The ship is using her aft derrick to tranship cargo into the barge alongside her stern, the barge at the bow being sheeted over ready for the journey further upriver.

Malcolm Cranfield

CUSTODIAN (8847/61) anchored in the Delaware River on arrival at Philadelphia from Port of Spain on 29th June 1977. She is a near-sister to the ADVENTURER.

Malcolm Cranfield Collection

The stern view on the same occasion shows the 110 ton capacity Stülcken heavy lift gear serving holds 3 and 4 amidships to good advantage.

Malcolm Cranfield Collection

CUSTODIAN (8847/61) leaving the locks at Eastham on 15th May 1979. She was sold out of Harrison service three months later, and her career came to a sad end in February 1982 when she was scuttled, having struck a reef off the Bahamas.

Laurie Schofield

DALESMAN (7200/61) approaching Eastham on 15th October 1977. Unusually for Harrison, she was built in the Netherlands by Nederlansche Dok-en-Scheepsbouw, Amsterdam.

Dave Gallichan, Bernard McCall Collection

DIPLOMAT (8202/53) leaves the Manchester Ship Canal at Eastham and enters the River Mersey in August 1969. Industrial Ellesmere Port ca
be seen on the right of the photograph.

Bernard McCall Collectio

DIPLOMAT (8202/53) arrives at Avonmouth on 23rd July 1972. This was one of her last voyages for Harrison, being sold to Cypriot owners later that year.

the late John Wiltshire courtesy Chris Howell, Malcolm Cranfield Collection

DISCOVERER (6162/64) sits high out of the water in this April 1972 view in the Port of London. She was the first of a class of five sisterships built in Gothenburg, Sweden.

Andrew Wiltshire Collection

DISCOVERER (6162/64) in the Liverpool dock system during the long hot summer of 1976. A year later she was sold to China and renamed JIN CHANG.

Laurie Schofield

EXPLORER (7200/61) leaving Cape Town with the unmistakeable backdrop of Table Mountain. This was the first vessel that had been built fo
Harrison Line by a shipyard outside the UK since the 1920s.

EXPLORER at Liverpool in summer 1976. The ship was sold to Liberian owners in 1978, but one wonders what has happened to the Merseyside Food Products Ltd offices on the right of the picture in the intervening years?

Laurie Schofield

FACTOR (6533/48) at Avonmouth. This ship spent her entire career with Harrison, being sold in March 1972 for demolition in Spain.

the late Richard Parsons courtesy of John D Hill, Malcolm Cranfield Collection

FORESTER (8377/52) leaves the Manchester Ship Canal at Eastham on 30th August 1969. She was Harrison's last steamship. Note the Mersey Ferries cruise vessel in the background.

Danny Lynch, Andrew Wiltshire Collection

In the King's Dock at Swansea, we see the GOVERNOR (6026/52) in 1969. In the same year, this ship was trapped in Manchester when the MANCHESTER COURAGE demolished the lock gates at Irlam on the Manchester Ship Canal.

the late John Wiltshir

HISTORIAN (8454/68) approaching the locks at Eastham with masts lowered ready for transit of the Manchester Ship Canal in 1976.

Dave Gallichan / Bernard McCall Collection

HISTORIAN (8454/68) at Swansea on 10th July 1970. Unusually she was berthed on the south side of the King's Dock. She was another heavy lift ship, with 150 ton Stülcken derricks serving the main holds.

the late John Wiltshire

Moving across the Dock, and HISTORIAN (8454/68) is berthed on the more usual north side of the King's Dock at Swansea. She was sold to Singaporean owners in 1981, and scrapped in Bangladesh in 1985.

the late John Wiltshire

INVENTOR (6210/35) alongside Market Street Wharf at New Orleans in the late 1950s. This is the oldest ship featured in this book, and is in the twilight of her career in this picture being sold for scrap in Belgium in 1960.

Malcolm Cranfield Collection

INVENTOR (9171/64) at Durban. This is a development of the ADVENTURER / CUSTODIAN design of heavy lift vessel. Like the HISTORIAN, she was sold to Singaporean owners in 1981. She was scrapped in Taiwan in 1985.

Trevor Jones, Malcolm Cranfield Collection

These two views show the extent of preparations required for the heavy-lift equipped INVENTOR (9171/64) to transit the Manchester Ship Canal. Here she approaches Eastham.

Dave Gallichan, Bernard McCall Collection

Having passed our photographers (who were standing next to each other!), the INVENTOR (9171/64) heads for the locks with tug assistance being provided by one of the Mersey's Alexandra fleet.

Bernard McCall

Another pair of views of the INVENTOR (9171/64), on this occasion being towed through the dock system at Avonmouth.

Stuart Kirkby, Bernard McCall Collection

And here she enters the locks, towed by the SEA MERRIMAC, with another of the CJ King fleet on her stern.

Stuart Kirkby, Bernard McCall Collection

JOURNALIST (8366/54) in London's Royal Docks in April 1972. A year later she was sold to Cypriot owners and, following further service under various flags, she was broken up in Pakistan in 1982.

C C Beazley, Andrew Wiltshire Collection

LINGUIST (6448/66) heading up the River Clyde. She ran aground and broke up on the Canadian coast in 1983, three years after leaving Harrison service.

Alastair Paterson, Andrew Wiltshire Collection

MAGICIAN (8454/68) at Middlesbrough on 16th January 1980. A sistership to the HISTORIAN, she joined her sister in being sold to Singapore in 1981, and was scrapped in India in 1985.

Michael Greer.

MAGICIAN (8454/68) at Avonmouth on 14th July 1969. She is transshipping some of her cargo to the coaster YEWFOREST alongside.

the late John Wiltshire

MERCHANT (5837/64) at Aberdeen on 3rd January 1979. She did not have long to go in Harrison service as she was laid up at Leith shortly afterwards, and was sold to Liberia later in the year.

Alastair Paterson, Andrew Wiltshire Collection

MERCHANT (5837/64) arriving at Eastham. This vessel was unusual in being purchased second hand by Harrison. She had begun life as Cunard's SCYTHIA.

Jim Shaw Collection courtesy of Trevor Jones, Malcolm Cranfield Collection

A number of T&J Harrison's vessels were sold to China at the end of their service with the company. On 4th September 1977, the NATURALIST (6162/65) was in the process of being repainted by her new owners at Middlesbrough.

Michael Green

With her change of identity completed, the former NATURALIST (6162/65) departs from Middlesbrough on 7th September 1977, now named YICHANG.

Michael Green

Sistership to the NATURALIST was the NOVELIST (6162/65) seen approaching Eastham, which followed her sister to China in 1977, as the WU CHANG.

Bernard McCall Collection

PHILOSOPHER (6162/64) at Liverpool on 15th March 1969. She was another sistership to head east in 1977, with her new Chinese owners renaming her YONG CHANG.

the late John Wiltshire

Two views of PLAINSMAN (8732/1959) approaching Latchford Locks on the Manchester Ship Canal.
Bernard McCall

PLAINSMAN (8732/59) in the Mersey, heading for Manchester, on 18th September 1970. She was the last of the three ship ADMINISTRATOR class.

the late John Wiltshire

The World War II built PROSPECTOR (6202/43) at Liverpool. She only survived in Harrison service for 18 years, being sold to Panamanian owners in 1961, and scrapped in Japan in 1962.

Russell Priest Collection, Malcolm Cranfield Collection

SCHOLAR (5837/65) leaving Aberdeen in October 1976. She is the second of the two Cunard vessels bought in 1969, having originally been that company's SAMARIA.

Alastair Paterson, Andrew Wiltshire Collection

SCHOLAR (5837/65) outbound from London passes Erith in June 1975. In 1980, a year after leaving Harrison ownership, she was trapped in the Shatt-el-Arab waterway by the start of the Iran-Iraq War, and sustained damage from shellfire.

Dave Salisbury, Malcolm Cranfield Collection

STATESMAN (6162/64) on the River Clyde in June 1972. This was the second of the five Gothenburg-built ships, delivered in 1964.

W D Harris, Andrew Wiltshire Collection

STATESMAN (6162/64) at Swansea on 10th June 1969. Like her sisterships, she was sold to China in 1977, becoming JIAN CHANG. She sank off the coast of Vietnam in 1990. The tug is the FORMBY of Alexandra Towing.

the late John Wiltshire

TACTICIAN (8844/61) in London's Royal Docks in June 1972. The vessel's heavy lift derricks have clearly been in use, with a special load atop No. 3 hold.

C C Beazley, Andrew Wiltshire Collection

The TRADER (6448/66) was a sistership to the LINGUIST. She was sold to Thai owners in 1980, and demolished in Thailand in 1986.

the late Les Ring, Andrew Wiltshire Collection

WANDERER (8150/51) at Swansea on 28th June 1969. She was sold a year later to Cypriot owners, for whom she worked for another four years
before a further sale to Panama, which was shortly followed by a one way trip to South Korean shipbreakers.

the late John Wiltshire, Malcolm Cranfield Collection

WAYFARER (8150/51) in the Mersey. She was sold to Cypriot owners after twenty years of service, but less than two years after leaving the Harrison fleet, she caught fire and ran aground on the Romanian coast. She was subsequently scrapped.

Roy Cressey Collection

INDEX

COVER PICTURES

Front: BENEFACTOR (11299/70) arrives at Avonmouth on 20th April 1976.

the late John Wiltshire

Back: Harrison's traditional black / white / red funnel colours as worn by the DIPLOMAT (8202/53) at Avonmouth on 23rd July 1972.

the late John Wiltshire

ACKNOWLEDGEMENTS

Sources used in the preparation of this book were *Harrisons of Liverpool*, published by Ships in Focus and the World Ship Society, and various issues of *Lloyd's Register* and *Marine News*.

In addition, I would like to thank **the photographers** who have kindly given access to their material for use in this book; **Coastal Shipping** and **HPC Publishing** for their ongoing encouragement and support **Sarah-Jane**, my ever-patient wife, for her continued unstinting support and encouragement.